Monsters in Greek Mythology

Titles in the *Library of Greek Mythology* series include:

Monsters in Greek Mythology

Don Nardo

San Diego, CA

© 2017 ReferencePoint Press, Inc.
Printed in the United States

For more information, contact:
ReferencePoint Press, Inc.
PO Box 27779
San Diego, CA 92198
www.ReferencePointPress.com

LIBRARY OF CONGRESS CATALOGING-IN-PUBLICATION DATA

Names: Nardo, Don, 1947- author.
Title: Monsters in Greek mythology / by Don Nardo.
Description: San Diego : ReferencePoint Press, 2016. | Series: The Library of
    Greek mythology series | Includes bibliographical references and index.
Identifiers: LCCN 2015039814 (print) | LCCN 2016006244 (ebook) | ISBN
    9781601529701 (hardback) | ISBN 9781601529718 (epub)
Subjects: LCSH: Monsters. | Mythology, Greek.
Classification: LCC BL795.M65 N375 2016 (print) | LCC BL795.M65 (ebook) | DDC
    398.20938/01--dc23
LC record available at http://lccn.loc.gov/2015039814

Contents

Ancient Greece (Circa 500 BCE)

Introduction

Monsters Reflected in a Distorting Mirror

An ancient Greek traveler boarded a cargo ship in hopes it would take him to a distant city, where he planned to visit relatives he had not seen in many years. At first, the voyage was uneventful. But then a massive storm set in, and before long the howling winds and angry sea capsized the vessel.

The traveler awakened on the beach of an island he did not recognize. The nearby shattered hull of the cargo ship confirmed that he had been shipwrecked, and his first concern was to find food and water. He left the beach, headed inland, and soon found himself in a forest filled with towering oaks and much dense underbrush that made his journey slow and difficult.

Eventually, the man emerged into a more open, grassy area crisscrossed by dirt paths and there beheld a strange and startling sight. All along the paths stood statues of men and women in diverse poses. The traveler wondered: Who would create so many extremely realistic-looking sculptures and leave them strewn across the countryside?

Then he stopped short and held his breath as he recalled a disturbing story that he had heard as a child. It told of a remote island on the edge of the known world where the monstrous Gorgons dwelled. Sisters, their names were Stheno, meaning "strong"; Euryale, or "far jumper"; and Medusa, meaning "queen." It was said that they had big, sharp tusks, long tongues hanging from their drooling mouths, and hissing snakes for hair. Even worse, when a person gazed upon the deadliest of the three—Medusa—he or she rapidly turned to stone.

Now seeing the surrounding statues in a new light, the traveler realized they had once been living, breathing beings. It was clear that this was the Gorgons' island and that he must flee as fast as his legs could carry him. But it was already too late. As he turned to run, he saw a hideous head topped by squirming serpents and realized he was gazing directly at Medusa's fearsome face.

Within seconds the terrified man could feel sickening changes coursing through his organs and skin. Knowing full well what was happening, he strained with all his might to escape, but these efforts were fruitless. Soon his hardening tissues lost their life force, and he became merely the latest addition to Medusa's growing collection of petrified people.

Obsessed with Monsters Tales

Medusa's reign of terror eventually came to a bitter end, according to another ancient Greek myth, when a heroic human warrior named Perseus finally slew her. The story of the Gorgons and Medusa's demise are just two of many colorful tales about monsters that every classical Greek knew from a young age. Generally speaking, the modern term *classical Greeks* refers to Greece's inhabitants from the 600s through the 300s BCE. This was the period in which they created a cultural outburst of astonishing breadth and quality.

This achievement was most pronounced in Athens, the most populous and influential of the hundreds of Greek city-states (tiny nations, each built around a central town). In a remarkably short time span, the Athenians invented the theater and democracy; erected the Parthenon temple, later called history's most perfect structure; and produced the incomparable philosophers Socrates, Plato, and Aristotle. These and other crucial Greek accomplishments laid the foundations of Western, or European-based, society, which over time came to shape much of the modern world.

One of the cultural legacies the ancient Greeks passed on to later generations of Westerners is an extensive body of myths that remain widely popular today. Among them are stories not only about the world's creation and the exploits of gods and goddesses, but also about monsters and other fantastic creatures. In fact, it would not be an exaggeration to say that the Greeks were obsessed with tales about monsters.

Perseus takes his revenge on an unfriendly king by presenting him with the severed head of Medusa. Although the monster is dead, the king turns to stone when he looks at the head.

Many modern experts think this fascination for the grotesque and primitive in a sense balanced the Greek passion for order, civilization, and artistic beauty. According to this view, they recognized that order had once sprung from *dis*order and that one could not appreciate beauty and goodness without recognizing the existence of ugliness and evil. As University of Oxford scholar Peter Stewart puts it:

A recurring trait of Greek art is that monstrous creatures seem to be held up as a foil to the Greeks' concept of civilization— a sort of distorting mirror in which the Greeks could look at themselves. The Greeks seem to have found these monstrous or semi-human creatures useful to explore and express their world-view, their ideas about humanity and civilization, the mortal and divine. Fantastical beings were part of the furniture of the Greek mind.[1]

In addition to the repellent Gorgons, those beings included one-eyed giants, huge snakes, multiheaded dragons, flying fiends with female faces, and numerous other horrors.

Myths Based on Fact?

The Greeks did not think those mythical creatures still existed in their own time. Rather, they held that the monsters, along with the humans and other characters in the myths, walked the earth many centuries before the classical era. The Greeks envisioned that distant past as "a time when the world was young," the late, noted scholar Edith Hamilton explained. In those days, she went on, "people had a connection with the earth, with trees, and seas, and flowers, and hills, unlike anything we ourselves can feel. When the stories were being shaped, we are given to understand, little distinction had as yet been made between the real and the unreal. The imagination was vividly alive and not checked by reason."[2]

The Greeks called that earlier age when "unreal" monsters supposedly roamed the world the Age of Heroes. The name derived from the belief that the monsters were often confronted and killed by bold, valiant warriors. Larger than life, compared to ordinary people, those heroes—like the monsters they fought—were also thought to frequently interact with the gods whom the classical Greeks worshipped.

Because most Greeks believed those events really occurred, they did not view their myths as made-up stories that mainly entertained people or taught moral lessons, as people view myths today. Historians John Camp and Elizabeth Fisher point out, "The classical Greeks believed these legends and regarded them as a part of their history." Modern experts differ on how many of those myths were based on fact. But there is no doubt, Camp and Fisher say, "that archaeology has provided numerous instances where myth and historical reality seem to coincide."[3]

The Age of Bronze

One major way the Greek myths and history coincided is that the Age of Heroes roughly corresponded with a real historical period. Scholars call it the late Bronze Age and date it from about 1600 to 1100 BCE. The name comes from the fact that tools and weapons were then made primarily of bronze, an alloy of copper and tin.

Historians now know that during that period, mainland Greece and its nearby islands were inhabited by two culturally advanced *ethne*, Greek for "distinct peoples." The Minoans, a name coined by modern scholars, occupied the islands, especially the largest Greek island, Crete. Meanwhile, mainland Greece supported several small competing kingdoms established by a people that historians call the Mycenaeans.

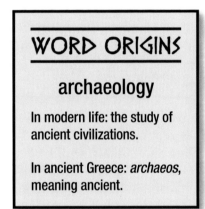

WORD ORIGINS

archaeology

In modern life: the study of ancient civilizations.

In ancient Greece: *archaeos*, meaning ancient.

Evidence indicates that the Minoans and Mycenaeans thrived for a few centuries. Then, in the decades following 1200 BCE, both peoples' realms fell apart for reasons that are still uncertain, and Greece swiftly descended into a cultural dark age. People sank into poverty, abandoned their palaces and other large buildings, stopped keeping written records, and eventually lost the ability to read and write. The formerly prosperous towns were replaced by "tiny unfortified settlements," Camp and Fisher write. Typically such a village consisted of "a handful of small houses built with rubble walls and mud, a poor and uninspired [collection] of pottery, no luxury goods, and a subsistence economy."[4]

A More Primitive Past

As a result of these major changes, Greece's former civilization passed into legend. Memories of the past society and its nations, achievements, wars, and leaders grew more and more disjointed or exaggerated over time. In many cases, those recollections gradually morphed into myths. Some of those tales featured frightening monsters, which were either based on mangled memories of real creatures and natural forces or were products of storytellers' imaginations.

Indeed, later Greek myth-tellers—like the famous eighth-century-BCE poet Homer—likely used their own inventiveness to fill in any gaps in the old stories. Such talented individuals, known as bards, were common in the 700s BCE, when Greece was regaining prosperity and rising from the Dark Age. They traveled far and wide, telling and retelling the tales about monsters, along with other myths, and in the process shaped and refined them. Those myths became an important aspect of the classical Greek culture that gradually emerged in the centuries that followed.

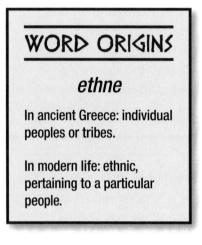

WORD ORIGINS

ethne

In ancient Greece: individual peoples or tribes.

In modern life: ethnic, pertaining to a particular people.

On the surface, that magnificent culture was all about humans and their strivings for political freedom, artistic perfection, and understanding of humanity's true place in the world. Giants, dragons, and other fearsome monsters were conspicuously absent. Yet beneath Greek society's ordered, seemingly sane surface lurked remnants of a more primitive past in which horrible creatures threatened people at every turn. In Peter Stewart's words, their myths about monsters showed that "their society was shaped by strange and primal forces as much as the guiding light of reason."[5]

Chapter One

Monsters from When the World Was New

L ike numerous other peoples in history, the ancient Greeks had myths about strange and terrifying monsters that supposedly lived in prior centuries. Some of those vile beasts were said to have emerged in primeval, or very ancient, times when the world was new and still forming. The Greeks had several different creation tales. But the most widely accepted one claimed that the universe, which the Greeks called the *kosmos* (today spelled *cosmos*), arose from Chaos, an immense, swirling mixture of various elements.

In a sense, Chaos itself was alive. It could not think, wonder about itself, or make decisions—so clearly, it lacked intelligence. Yet it nevertheless possessed the spark of life. Because it was always shifting and changing form, and also because it was raw, powerful, and dangerous, Chaos was not just the first being that the ancient Greeks believed came into existence. Also in their eyes, it was the first monster.

Other living things eventually emerged from churning Chaos, as if it had given birth to them. One was Gaea, Mother Earth, whose huge body consisted of all the world's landforms. Another was Uranus, the sky god. A third enormous being that sprang from Chaos was the second monster to be born. Called Tartarus, its dark recesses sprawled deep below Gaea's hulking mass.

Not long after they appeared, Gaea and Uranus proceeded to mate, and many of their offspring were plainly monstrous. Some had multiple heads or arms or were otherwise malformed or bizarre. Others looked much like people would when the gods later created humanity.

Except that these first humanoid, or human-shaped, creatures were Cyclopes—ugly brutes each having a single eye in the center of its forehead.

Gaea also mated with Tartarus. This strange coupling produced still another monster—Echidna, which ancient writers described as having a woman's head and a snake's body. Whatever these primeval monsters looked like, almost all of them had one thing in common. Namely, they were gigantic in comparison to people.

Fear of the Unknown?

It is only natural to wonder why the classical Greeks, who included both highly educated and poorly educated people, believed that those huge and frightening beings had once existed. The answer to that question is not yet fully understood. But most modern experts think that the handful of scientists and other highly educated individuals in Greek society likely doubted that such creatures had been real.

WORD ORIGINS

gigantic

In modern life: huge.

In ancient Greece: *gigas*, meaning "very large."

Indeed, beginning with the thinkers Thales and Anaximander in the 600s and 500s BCE, Greece produced the world's first philosopher-scientists. Several of them broke with earlier notions that lofty, all-powerful gods created and controlled the universe. Those deities might exist, some of the scientists said. But if so, they dwelled far away from earth and had no interest in or contact with humanity.

Similarly, the existence of huge monsters with the power to destroy the natural order, like some of those in the myths, seemed far-fetched to the early philosopher-scientists. For them it made more sense that nature operated by means of unthinking but powerful laws that were inherent in nature's very structure. "The great contribution of the sixth-century Greek thinkers," noted historian Sarah B. Pomeroy points out, was "their determination to abandon the mythological and religious framework and attempt instead to explain the world by material processes alone."[6]

The ancient Greeks saw Chaos, depicted in this eighteenth-century engraving, as a dangerous, ever-changing being. It was the first monster to populate their myths.

However, the majority of people in classical Greek society were far less educated than the philosopher-scientists. The average Greek tended to fall back on time-honored tales about the gods, the world's creation, the supernatural, and mythical monsters. Earlier, moreover, the inhabitants of Greece during the Dark Age (circa 1100 to 800 BCE), when the traditional Greek myths formed, lacked any education at all and were very gullible and superstitious.

Those early Greeks had not yet developed a scientific way of looking at the world. Nor were they able to map the world and explain how it worked. Moreover, they had a quite natural fear—*phobos* in their language—of what lurked in dark places and on remote islands.

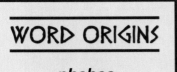

WORD ORIGINS

phobos

In ancient Greece: the word for "fear."

In modern life: phobia, meaning an unnatural fear of something.

That fear of the unknown led some people to imagine the existence of nightmarish beasts.

Another factor, undoubtedly, consisted of early travelers' tales of monstrous creatures. Many of those stories were likely based on highly exaggerated accounts of their encounters with ordinary animals they had never seen before. In addition, some reports surely derived from people finding skeletons of large extinct animals and assuming more of those "monsters" must still exist. Hence many myths became populated by three-headed dogs, giants, dragons, snake-haired women, demons, shape-shifters, and many other scary creatures.

Europe Shaken to Its Foundations

Among the most frightening of all those mythical monsters were the earliest to emerge in the period when the world was young. Many, the Greeks held, sprang from the union of Gaea and Uranus, the vast beings who represented the earth and sky. But Gaea also mated with another immense being who made up an entire region—black Tartarus. It lay beneath the underworld and in later mythology became the dismal prison for all sorts of nasty creatures, gods, and villains.

Gaea and Tartarus begot the monster Echidna, with its woman's head and serpentine body, but Echidna had siblings who were even more repulsive than she was. The most loathsome of the brood was Typhon, which one ancient Greek myth-teller described as

> a mixture of man and beast, the largest and strongest of all Gaea's children. Down to the thighs he was human in form, so large that he extended beyond all the mountains while his head often touched even the stars. One hand reached to the west, the other to the east, and attached to these were one hundred

heads of serpents. Also from the thighs down he had great coils of vipers, which extended to the top of his head and hissed mightily. All of his body was winged, and the hair that flowed in the wind from his head and cheeks was matted and dirty. In his eyes flashed fire. Such were the appearance and the size of Typhon as he hurled red-hot rocks at the sky itself, and set out for it with mixed hisses and shouts, as a great storm of fire boiled forth from his mouth.[7]

Cerberus's Best-Known Myth

Cerberus, the three-headed dog that guarded the perimeter of the underworld, was mentioned in several Greek myths. By far the best known was the one involving its capture by the famous muscleman Heracles (today better known as Hercules). A Greek ruler named Eurystheus ordered the hero to perform twelve seemingly impossible feats. One was to go down into the dark reaches of the underworld, snare the vicious Cerberus, and bring it back to Greece. After a treacherous journey, the obedient Heracles found the monstrous dog and slowly approached it. Cerberus watched the intruder warily with its six eyes (two in each of its three heads). After a while, the strongman felt the time was right and rushed at the beast, which leapt to one side, trying to avoid the charging man. But Heracles managed to snag one of the monster's hairy paws. Cerberus tripped and crashed to the ground, after which the two wrestled furiously, with barely a spare second to catch a breath, for more than an hour. Finally Heracles, who possessed phenomenal strength and endurance, overcame the exhausted giant canine. After caging Cerberus, the victor of the bout brought the captive creature to King Eurystheus. That monarch and his subjects marveled at the legendary monster for a while. Then Eurystheus acknowledged that Cerberus was too dangerous to keep and told Heracles to take it back to the underworld. Soon the monster was back where it belonged—guarding the borders of Hades's dimly lit realm.

Typhon appeared in several myths. But perhaps the most famous and exciting was the one in which his mother sent him to do battle with Zeus, leader of the Olympian gods. These were the deities worshipped by the classical Greeks. Gaea had a long-standing dislike for Zeus and had attempted, but always failed, to destroy him before. This time, however, she used her most formidable weapon—the enormous and powerful Typhon.

There was one notable flaw in Gaea's plan, however. Although Typhon was big and strong, like many of the Greek mythical monsters he was fairly dim-witted. So he did not know to approach his prey carefully in order to successfully ambush him. Feeling the ground tremble at Typhon's approach, the shrewd Zeus had plenty of time to prepare. The chief god prepared several of his trademark thunderbolts, his favorite weapon. Composed of pure electricity, such a bolt could shock and fry the tissues of any living thing, including the largest monsters.

Zeus suddenly leapt from hiding and tossed a thunderbolt at the surprised Typhon, who was disoriented by the blow and fell to his snake-infested knees. After a few minutes, the monstrous being rose back up and charged at his opponent. But Zeus, who was too quick for him, easily dodged to one side and while still in the air hurled three more sparkling bolts.

The battle went on for hours and shook the continent to its very foundations. One ancient account of the myth said that the terrible fight motivated various other deities to flee southward to Egypt. There they disguised themselves as animals, and the Greeks believed this was why so many Egyptian gods had the heads of beasts.

Eventually, Zeus was victorious. Having burned many of Typhon's body parts to a crisp, he hurled the monster down into the dark depths of Tartarus. Yet Typhon was not dead. Thereafter, the Greeks believed, he now and then expelled a massive breath, and those colossal rushes of air rose up from Tartarus. They became the large storms called hurricanes by some and typhoons, after Typhon, by others. This is an example of how the Greeks employed myths about mighty monsters to help explain certain large-scale natural events.

Hellhound and Faithful Guard Dog

Before his epic fight with Zeus, Typhon supposedly mated with its own sibling, Echidna, producing Cerberus. In most ancient accounts,

Cerberus, a giant doglike creature, had three heads. Another source—the seventh-century-BCE Greek epic poet Hesiod—claimed it had fifty heads. However, Hesiod agreed with all ancient writers about the beast's singular role: to guard the borders of the underworld and ensure that no shades, or souls, who entered that realm ever escaped. Cerberus was "a dreaded hound," Hesiod wrote, "who has no pity." For any zombielike shade who attempted to leave that dimly lit subterranean realm, the vicious hellhound "lies in wait for them and eats them up."[8]

The giant three-headed doglike beast known as Cerberus guards the borders of the underworld. According to Greek mythology, anyone who attempts to leave that realm comes face to face with the vicious hellhound.

With Eyes Like Fire

Several ancient Greek and Roman authors described the weird and frightening griffins that were said to dwell in both Scythia and further eastward in India. One of them, the second-century-CE Roman writer Aelian, wrote:

> I have heard that the Indian animal the Griffin is a quadruped [four-footed creature] like a lion; that it has claws of enormous strength and that they resemble those of a lion. Men commonly report that it is winged and that the feathers along its back are black, and those on its front are red, while the actual wings are neither but are white. And [the fifth-century-BCE Greek historian] Ctesias records that its neck is variegated [multicolored] with feathers of a dark blue; that it has a beak like an eagle's, and a head too, just as artists portray it in pictures and sculpture. Its eyes, he says, are like fire. It builds its lair among the mountains, and although it is not possible to capture the full-grown animal, they do take the young ones. And the people of Bactria, who are neighbors of the Indians, say that the Griffins guard the gold in those parts; that they dig it up and build their nests with it, and that the Indians carry off any that falls from them. The Indians however deny that they guard the aforesaid gold, for the Griffins have no need for it.

Aelian, *On Animals,* trans. A.F. Scholfield, excerpted in Theoi Greek Mythology, "Grypes." www.theoi.com.

That the classical Greeks envisioned a monstrous canine creature guarding the edges of the underworld might at first glance seem as though they feared or disliked dogs. But the reality was quite different. First, ordinary dogs, including hunting hounds and personal companions to gods and people, were mentioned in dozens of Greek myths. Artemis, goddess of animals and the hunt, for example, was said to keep numerous hunting dogs. Greek artists frequently depicted her with several of them at her side. There is also the human king Odysseus's dog, Argus, in the *Odyssey*, by the renowned eighth-century-BCE Greek epic poet Homer. In one of the most touching scenes in all of Western literature, after being away from home for twenty years, Odysseus returns to find the faithful animal still waiting patiently for him.

Also, in their daily lives many classical Greeks enjoyed the company of dogs and kept them in their homes, as numerous people do today. Xanthippus, father of the famous fifth-century-BCE Athenian democratic reformer Pericles, was particularly fond of his dog. So he made sure that when the pup died, its remains were placed beside his own in his tomb. In that same century the noted Athenian thinker Socrates argued that dogs had the unique ability to know which people were true and good friends. That, he stated, made those animals ideal companions for humans and worthy of the utmost respect.

This respect for canines actually extended to Cerberus. Although the Greeks looked on him as a monster to be feared, they also viewed him as a benefactor of sorts. Many residents of the classical Greek world feared the spirits of the dead. It was thought that such ghosts occasionally escaped from the underworld and haunted the living. Thus, by ensuring that most shades did not leave that underground realm, Cerberus did society a service. He was therefore a faithful guard dog as well as a monster.

Guarding the Gold

The Greeks believed that other monsters from when the world was young lurked on the edges of the known world. Among them were exceedingly strange-looking creatures called griffins. Several classical Greek writings mention them, and Greek artists often portrayed them in wall paintings and scenes decorating vases, bowls, and other ceramic objects.

The popular belief was that a griffin possessed the torso of a lion and the head, beak, and wings of an eagle. The first- to second-century-CE Greek writer Philostratus described the creatures, saying, "In size and strength they resemble lions. But having this advantage over them that they have wings, they will attack them, and they get the better of elephants and of dragons. But they have no great power of flying, not more than have birds of short flight, for they are not winged as is proper with birds, but the palms of their feet are webbed with red membranes."[9]

Griffins were not thought to hunt humans as prey, as many mythical monsters did. Instead, the beasts supposedly sniffed out caches of treasure, especially gold. Then they carefully guarded the loot to make sure greedy people did not steal it.

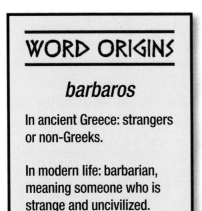

WORD ORIGINS

barbaros

In ancient Greece: strangers or non-Greeks.

In modern life: barbarian, meaning someone who is strange and uncivilized.

Ancient accounts of griffins derive from a large region stretching from eastern Europe through the Middle East to India. But the area the Greeks most associated them with was Scythia (now Ukraine), then a sparsely populated territory lying well north of Greece. The *barbaros*, or non-Greeks, who dwelled in the region claimed to have found some remains of the creatures. They and a few Greek traders also reported that a few griffins had been seen in the flesh.

The Beast Who Stood for Fear

Like the majority of the earliest Greek mythical monsters, the griffin was a hybrid creature—that is, a combination of two or more living species. The same was true of one of the most famous of all legendary monsters—the Minotaur. Featuring the head of a bull and the body of a man, it dwelled in a large maze of rocky corridors and chambers— the Labyrinth—lying beneath a palace. That royal abode belonged to Minos, king of the large island of Crete during the early years of the Age of Heroes.

The Minotaur did Minos's bidding, and in their best-known myth they terrorized the then-small town of Athens, situated on the nearby Greek mainland. Minos's beloved son had died while in Athens, and Minos unjustly blamed the city's ruler, Aegeus, for the loss. Intending to achieve vengeance, the more powerful Cretan king forced Aegeus to go along with a mean-spirited and plainly one-sided deal. During every ninth year, the Athenians had to send fourteen young people—

seven males and seven females—to Crete. There, Minos eagerly handed them over to the always hungry, flesh-eating Minotaur.

Eventually, this awful arrangement was eliminated by Aegeus's valiant son, Theseus. The young man volunteered to go to Crete and save the Athenian hostages from certain death in the Labyrinth. Once in the Minotaur's lair, Theseus fought and slew the bestial bull-man, and Minos's cruel stranglehold over Athens was over.

The Minotaur, which has the head of a bull and the body of a man, finally meets its match in a battle for survival. It is just one of many monsters with physical features from more than one species.

For the classical Athenians, this myth of man versus monster was part of a larger set of very ancient stories involving Theseus, whom they still looked on as the city's national hero. In their eyes, he was not merely an entertaining character in a quaint old tale. Rather, they were certain he was a real person of uncommon courage who had made classical Athens possible.

Not only had Theseus killed the Minotaur and ended their city's political servitude to Crete, the myths claimed, he had also returned home and unified Athens with the scattered villages and towns surrounding it. The result was the creation of a powerful political unit that over many centuries became Greece's most populous and influential city-state.

Thus, the classical Athenians viewed the myth of the monstrous Minotaur as a potent part of their national history. But had a creature half man and half bull actually existed? Many average Athenians and other ancient Greeks assumed it had.

Meanwhile, the intellectuals of the day, including philosopher-scientists like Plato (circa 424 to 348 BCE), were more inclined to see such mythical monsters as symbols of natural forces or human feelings. In Plato's time, the Athenians still observed a national celebration of Theseus's slaying of the Minotaur. For Plato, that beast was a fable that represented the quite normal human fear of death. This, he proposed, was the adult version of the childhood fear of monsters lurking in the darkness. In his dialogue *Phaedo*, one of his friends addresses their real-life mentor, the older philosopher Socrates, saying, "Socrates, you must argue us out of our fears. And yet, strictly speaking, they are not *our* fears, but [rather] there is a child within [each of] us to whom death is a sort of goblin [monster]. Him too we must persuade not to be afraid when he is alone in the dark."[10] Whether or not they believed that the monsters from their myths had been real, the Greeks strongly felt the influence of those old stories in their daily lives.

Chapter Two

The Brutish Cyclopes and Other Giants

M any of the Greek myths featured giants of one sort of another. Some of those monstrous beings were bigger than others. They could be as tall as a temple, like the famous Parthenon, the ruins of which still grace Athens's central hill, the Acropolis. Others were so huge that when lying on the ground they covered many acres. One thing true about *all* the mythical giants, however, was that even the smallest ones easily towered over humans.

The reasons that the classical Greeks perpetuated so many tales about giants remains somewhat uncertain. But most modern scholars suggest that Greek thinkers and writers were captivated by how human society fit into nature's overall scheme. They recognized that large-scale natural events—like earthquakes, storms, and floods—periodically killed many people and destroyed their works.

The giants in the myths often affected human society in similar destructive ways. So it may be that in the classical Greek mind those enormous legendary creatures symbolized, or stood for, earthquakes and other natural forces. Indeed, one of the chief themes employed by ancient Greek writers and artists was an ongoing struggle between humanity and nature's violent tendencies. This theme was also sometimes couched in terms of ordered human society versus primitive, barbaric forces. In Greek mythology, scholar Charles Freeman states, when either the Greek gods or ordinary Greeks defeat giants, "a point is being made. It is that the cunning Greek can triumph over a monstrous brute."[11]

Two Major Cyclopean Traditions

This recurring concept of civilization battling primitivism is plainly visible in the tales of the most familiar of all the Greek mythical giants—the Cyclopes. They resembled humans in that they had a torso with a head, two arms, and two legs. One glaring difference between the two species, however, was that each Cyclops had a single eye in the middle of its forehead.

Not all Cyclopes were alike. The classical Greeks inherited a number of different traditions, or story lines, concerning these beings. One popular tradition derived from Hesiod, the well-to-do seventh-century-BCE Greek farmer who also wrote epic poetry. In his long work titled *Theogony*, he said that in the earliest times Gaea (Mother Earth) and Uranus (Father Heaven) mated to produce three one-eyed giants. Their names were Brontes (Thunderer), Arges (Shiner), and Steropes (Lightning Maker).

Uranus feared these huge offspring of his. His main worry was that they might turn on him and try to dislodge him from his powerful position in the natural order. So one by one he captured the Cyclopes and locked them up in the dark and dismal depths of Tartarus.

Later, another brood of Gaea's and Uranus's children—the Titans, the first race of Greek gods—fought a younger race of deities, the Olympians, for mastery of the cosmos. The leader of the Olympians, mighty Zeus, wisely freed Brontes, Arges, and Steropes from their underground prison. They helped him defeat the Titans by fashioning weapons for the Olympians. These tools included the potent thunderbolts that Zeus famously hurled at his enemies and the trident, a three-pronged spear wielded by Zeus's brother, Poseidon, ruler of the seas.

Numerous Greek and later Roman writers described the majestic forges at which these Cyclopes worked their wonders, first for Zeus and later for Hephaestos, the blacksmith god. The first-century-BCE Roman poet Virgil placed those forges beneath an island on the southern Italian coast, saying that the place's "cliffs, sheer-rising, jet out smoke from their crannies. Deep within it are vaults, a rumbling volcanic cavern scooped out by the action of the Cyclopes' fires. You can hear the clang of hard blows on the anvils, the roaring when masses of ore are smelted within, and a throbbing blast of flame from the furnaces. Here is Hephaestos's place. The island is called Volcania."[12]

Another ancient tradition about giant Cyclopes pictures a race of them hailing from Thrace, the region bordering the Aegean Sea's northern edge. According to the myth, in ancient times a part of that rugged, sparsely populated area was the home of a tribe of huge men who had but one eye each. For reasons that are unclear, they migrated into southern Greece. There they earned their keep by erecting walls, palaces, and citadels for local human rulers. These structures were supposedly impregnable to attack because they were composed of gigantic stones that no one but the Cyclopes could lift.

So-Called Proof for the Cyclopes

To the classical Greeks, these stories about one-eyed giants were not merely entertaining folktales. First, various farmers, miners, and others who regularly dug beneath the ground sometimes found what most

The skull of an extinct elephant that lived in Greece millions of years ago (pictured) has a spherical pit in the center where the trunk would have been. Knowing little about the world before their time, the ancient Greeks took this as proof of the existence of the Cyclopes.

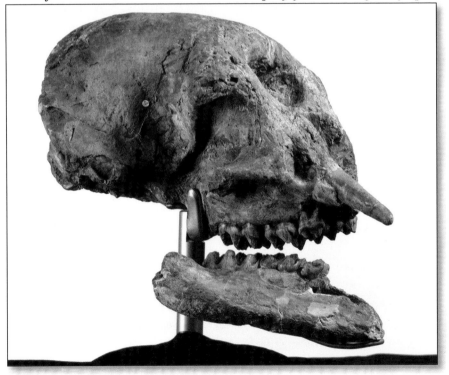

Myth-Tellers' Corner: Homer

The ancient Greeks frequently referred to Homer simply and almost reverently as "the poet," a tribute to his status as the finest writer their civilization had ever produced. Even the Greeks of the fifth-century-BCE cultural golden age no longer recalled when and where Homer was born. Today a majority of scholars think he hailed from the Aegean island of Chios sometime in the 700s BCE.

Homer was one of a long line of bards who both composed and recited epic poems—long, serious tales told in verse. It appears that he created the final versions of two magnificent epics that had been passed down to him from earlier bards. One, the *Iliad,* describes a series of events near the end of the well-known mythical Trojan War; the second epic, the *Odyssey,* follows the adventures of Odysseus, the cleverest of the Greek kings who besieged Troy.

Homer's origins are not the only things about him that remain uncertain. Did he compose both epics, just one, or neither? If he did not write, or at least finalize them, then who did? Was he even a real person? Modern experts have combined these and other similar mysteries about Homer and his life into a body of intense literary inquiry usually referred to as the "Homeric question."

Classical Greek thinkers and writers also debated those questions. They were unable to come to any definite conclusions. But they could not deny that the two Homeric epics had a tremendous influence on Greek society, customs, and thought.

people viewed as tangible proof that such giants had once existed. This evidence took the form of very large skeletons of creatures that had clearly once walked the earth. In particular, each skeleton featured a skull that had a large circular pit in its center. This must be where the giant's single eye was once attached, people reasoned.

This analysis of the skeletons and skulls turned out to be erroneous, however. Modern scientists discovered that those widely distributed bones belonged to an extinct form of elephant that had lived in Greece millions of years ago. The spherical pit in the middle of each skull was where the animal's trunk was attached.

Modern experts also point out a probable reason why the Greeks developed myths about Cyclopes who operated forges, like those who supposedly worked for Zeus and Hephaestos. That image of one-eyed blacksmiths may well have been a distorted memory of real blacksmiths handed down through the generations from the Bronze Age to the classical era. Evidence shows that Bronze Age Greek smiths wore patches over one eye in order to prevent sparks from the forge from blinding them. Over the course of centuries, including the Dark Age when knowledge passed only by word of mouth, this singular image could well have given rise to tales about one-eyed forge operators.

As for the race of mythical Cyclopes who built huge stone walls and palaces, the classical Greeks felt the evidence for their existence lay across the southern Greek mainland. That evidence consisted of the ruins of very ancient structures made of immense stones each weighing dozens or even hundreds of tons. Of those ruins, the most impressive examples were the imposing fortresses at Argos, Tiryns, and Mycenae, all in southern Greece. Surely, the common thinking went, only a race of giants could have lifted those tremendous stones into place. Speaking of the fortress at Tiryns, the second-century-CE Greek traveler Pausanias said it "was built by Cyclopes with natural rocks, all so huge that a pair of mules would not even begin to shift the smallest!"[13]

But what the Greeks of classical times did not realize was that the structures in question were remains of Bronze Age palace-citadels erected by the Mycenaeans. They had moved the stones by combining mechanical hoists with the muscle power of dozens of oxen and other animals. The problem was that the later Greeks had no memory (*mnestis* in their language) of the Mycenaeans and associated what had really been an earlier Greek era with the imaginary Age of Heroes.

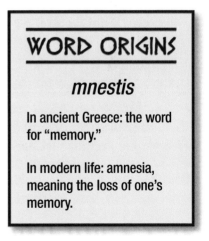

WORD ORIGINS

mnestis

In ancient Greece: the word for "memory."

In modern life: amnesia, meaning the loss of one's memory.

Homer's Island Cyclopes

The Greeks had still another tradition about giant Cyclopes, this one established mainly in Homer's epic poem the *Odyssey*. That work tells of the wanderings of the hero Odysseus, one of the Greek kings who helped besiege the legendary city of Troy. After Troy fell, Odysseus and his men sailed for Greece. But a terrible storm blew them off course, and in time they landed on a remote island inhabited by one-eyed giants.

Odysseus later recalled (in Homer's words) that those Cyclopes were "a fierce, uncivilized people, who never lift a hand to plant or plow," and therefore had no *agros*, or tilled land. They also had no "laws, nor any settled customs," Odysseus said, "but live in hollow caverns in the mountain heights, where each man is lawgiver to his children and his wives, and nobody cares a jot for his neighbors."[14]

Odysseus took twelve men and went ashore to search for food and water. Finding a big cave filled with goats and sheep, they started to take some of the animals but were interrupted by the cave's owner, the Cyclops Polyphemus. He blocked the entrance with a large rock, trapping the intruders inside. Over the course of two days, the giant killed and ate several of Odysseus's men. The survivors managed to defeat Polyphemus by driving a sharpened pole into his single eye and thereby blinding him. Then they tricked the lumbering ogre, who was something of a moron, into rolling back the rock, and made their escape.

On one level, the classical Greeks viewed the widely popular myth of the Cyclops Polyphemus as entertainment, part of the exciting adventure story Homer presented in the *Odyssey* as a whole. But on a deeper level they accepted the tale as a kind of life lesson. Through his two great epics, Homer taught the later classical Greeks much about how to live in and manage a functioning society. In this case he showed them a model of what did and did not constitute civilized behavior. The Cyclopes on the island, researcher Frank Redmond

WORD ORIGINS

agros

In ancient Greece: tilled land, or farmland.

In modern life: agriculture, the practice of tilling land and farming.

Odysseus and his men escape after driving a sharpened pole into the one eye of the Cyclops Polyphemus. Blinded, the giant could no longer keep his captives locked inside his cave.

explains, "live in a state of absolute anarchy where each man is for himself. Because they lack a centralized assembly of law and culture, the Cyclopes cannot reap the benefits of civilization, namely leisure and pleasures. Instead they will perpetually [live] aloof in their own lawless ways."[15]

In contrast, the *Odyssey* describes a highly civilized people that Odysseus encountered—the Phaeacians. The classical Greeks were well aware that that mythical people represented the Greeks themselves. "The Phaeacian way of life," compared to "the Cyclopean way of life," Redmond continues, "is structured, sophisticated, and harmonious—in a word, civilized. The Phaeacians live in a society where everything works together as a structured whole. Thus, their society is lawful and cultured, whereas the Cyclopes' is precisely the opposite."[16]

The Giants Against the Gods

Not all of the monstrous giants in Greek mythology were one-eyed. The earliest humanoid two-eyed giants in the myths were also the off-spring of Uranus, but not from a union with Gaea. Instead, Uranus's son, Cronos, attacked him and severed his genitals. The thousands of blood droplets scattered by this grue-some wound soon grew into an army of giants—the so-called Gigantes, who came under the sway of Gaea.

After Zeus and his Olympians defeated the first race of gods—Gaea's children, the Titans—and imprisoned them in Tartarus, Mother Earth fumed with rage. Hoping to free her offspring from Tartarus, she enlisted the newly formed tribe of Gigantes to aid her in an insurrection against Zeus and his fellow Olympians.

The classical Greeks called the great battle between the two powerful groups the Gigantomachy. During the furious fighting, the leader of the giants, Eurymedon, ripped off the top of a mountain and threw it at Zeus. Imitating this move, the other giants hurled massive boulders as well as trees they had uprooted. The Olympians managed to dodge most of those missiles, and in retaliation Zeus unleashed his signature thunderbolts. Eventually, Zeus and his followers won, and the giants who had not been killed in the fray ran for their lives. The Olympians celebrated what they viewed as a victory of civilized beings over barbaric monsters.

WORD ORIGINS

Odyssey

In ancient Greece: the title of Homer's epic poem about a hero's ten-year-long journey in search of his homeland.

In modern life: odyssey, meaning a long, event-filled journey.

"Nobody"

One of the highlights of the myth of the giant Cyclops Polyphemus, which Homer included in the epic poem the *Odyssey*, was an episode that emphasized his lack of intelligence. At the same time, it contrasted that dim-wittedness, an uncivilized quality, with the civilized cleverness of the story's hero, Odysseus, a Greek. After trapping the Greeks in the cave and eating several of them, the giant asked Odysseus to reveal his name. The shrewd Greek already had an escape plan in mind and therefore lied and said his name was "Nobody."

Later that evening, Polyphemus, who had had too much to drink, dozed off. At that moment Odysseus set the rest of his plan in motion. He and his surviving men used the tip of a sharpened pole to poke out the sleeping monster's single eye. After awakening with a start and screaming, the giant gathered the few wits he had and started calling for help from his fellow Cyclopes, who lived in nearby caves.

Sure enough, some of those ugly ogres gathered outside the big rock that blocked the cave entrance. They asked Polyphemus why he was making such a racket. Who had injured him, they inquired? The wounded giant then remembered the name Odysseus had told him earlier. Polyphemus repeatedly told them that "Nobody" had injured him. Hearing this, his neighbors decided that he was simply drunk and departed. Just as Odysseus had hoped, the Greeks' captor could no longer count on getting any outside help.

In the classical era and the centuries that immediately followed, the Greeks saw the Gigantomachy the same way but chose to celebrate that pivotal mythical event in their art. All over Greece, numerous paintings, sculptures, and mosaics depicted the battle. Of these works, the most striking example was the enormous band of sculptures that wound around the base of the great Altar of Zeus at Pergamum (in what is now western Turkey). It displayed seventy-five figures of giants and gods in the midst of the Gigantomachy. The surviving sections of the sculpture show that its creators achieved a truly astounding degree of realism. This and other similar artworks of the period made mythology come to life on a daily basis for the residents of all the Greek lands.

Mighty Zeus unleashes an attack on the Gigantes, or giants, during the great battle known to the classical Greeks as the Gigantomachy. Ultimately, Zeus and his followers triumphed.

Orion and Talos

Still other monstrous giants populated Greek mythology, several of them considerably larger than the Cyclopes and Gigantes. The biggest of all the mythical giants was Orion. Indeed, ancient accounts said he was taller than the oceans were deep. According to Virgil, "As great Orion moves forward, cleaving his way, with his feet treading the floor of the deepest mid-ocean, his shoulders . . . [rise above] the waves. When he's carrying back from the hills some venerable ash tree, walking upon the ground he buries his head in the cloud-base."[17]

Of the various myths about Orion, the best known tells how that accomplished hunter fell in love with one of the Pleiades. They were the seven daughters of the Titan Atlas, who was famous for holding part of the sky on his back. Orion pursued those maidens relentlessly, which eventually caught Zeus's attention. The ruler of the gods did not desire that the giant should actually catch the Pleiades, so he transformed both Orion and the young women into separate constellations, or star groups, in the night sky. The classical Greeks felt that this myth adequately explained how the two star groups got into the sky.

Another famous giant from the Greek myths was composed completely of bronze. Named Talos, he was said to guard the island of Crete from intruders. In his most famous tale, he encountered the Argonauts, the group of heroes who, led by the renowned Jason, found the fabulous Golden Fleece (the skin of a magical ram). Talos hurled huge boulders at the Argonauts' ship, the *Argo,* but missed. With the aid of Jason's recently acquired ally, Medea, the Argonauts finally managed to defeat and kill Talos.

Once again, as in so many other Greek mythical stories about giants and monsters, agents of Greek civilization were able to overcome primitive, extremely destructive forces. That theme, which runs throughout the classical Greeks' myths and writings, made them feel morally superior to other peoples. It also instilled in them an abundance of confidence that their future would be bright and limitless.

Chapter Three

Repulsive Reptilians Menace Society

The myths of the ancient Greeks were riddled with repulsive reptilian beasts. Some of these serpents and dragons walked or slithered on the ground, others had wings and flew through the air, and still others featured fins and swam in the seas. One thing they all had in common was that they were a menace to humans and civilized society.

The Greeks were not the only ancient or medieval people who had myths about dragons, serpents, and similar reptilelike monsters. The Chinese and Norse (Viking) mythologies are only two of the many others worldwide. This fact has long fascinated modern mythologists and scientists alike and inspired numerous theories to explain the phenomenon.

One of those scientists was the late Carl Sagan, who speculated about mythical reptilian monsters in his 1977 book, *The Dragons of Eden*. He acknowledged that numerous past cultures, from those of Greece, Egypt, and China to those of the ancient Americas, had myths about dangerous and threatening dragons or serpents. He suggested that buried deeply in the subconscious mind of all human beings is a sort of lingering memory of a period predating the development of civilization. In that primeval era, he wrote, primitive people were forced to struggle daily simply to escape the clutches of what were to them very real reptilian monsters. Sagan said, "Is it only an accident that the common human sounds commanding silence or attracting attention seem strangely imitative of the hissing of reptiles? Is it possible that dragons posed a problem for our proto-human ancestors of a few million years ago, and that the terror they evoked and the deaths they caused helped bring about the evolution of human intelligence?"[18]

A similar, more recent argument suggesting that early human brains became hard-wired to fear reptilelike predators was advanced by anthropologist David E. Jones in his 2002 book, *An Instinct for Dragons*. Sagan's and Jones's ideas on the subject have yet to be fully accepted by a majority of scientists. Yet they do seem to explain why the Greeks, Chinese, Egyptians, Persians, Norse, Celts, and other peoples of the past all had very similar tales about dragons, giant snakes, and other scary reptilian monsters.

The Fire-Breathing Chimera

Many of the dragons populating the world's myths could fly, and the classical Greeks believed that some of those winged beasts terrorized their ancestors. The most famous of the Greek flying reptilians was the deadly Chimera. It was one of Greek mythology's many composite creatures—those that combined features of several different species. According to Hesiod, the Chimera was "a beast great and terrible, and strong and swift-footed. Her heads were three. One was that of a glare-eyed lion, one of a goat, and the third of a snake, a powerful dragon." Furthermore, he wrote, the monster "snorted raging fire,"[19] a trait that would eventually become almost universal for legendary dragons.

The Chimera was supposedly one of the horrible offspring of the vile union of two of the earliest Greek mythical monsters—Typhon and Echidna. That fact alone ensured that the Chimera would be not only physically ugly but also mean-spirited and extremely dangerous. Indeed, according to the chief myth of that dragon, it had an insatiable appetite for human flesh. For many months the Chimera ravaged areas of Lycia, a part of what is now Turkey that in ancient times was occupied on and off by Greeks. The monster snatched up and devoured farmers in their fields and scorched whole villages with its red-hot breath.

At first, the story goes, no one dared try to stop the frightening flying dragon. But then a bold young man named Bellerophon stepped forward and offered to confront the beast. Someone advised him to first visit an elderly soothsayer, or wise man, named Polyeidus. If Bellerophon tried to fight the Chimera by himself, on foot, the old seer said, he would surely be killed. Instead, Polyeidus advised, the would-be dragon slayer should seek out the famous flying horse, Pegasus. The problem was that the handsome white steed was very elusive. It dwelled on the rugged slopes of Mount Helicon in central Greece and spent much of its time cruising the clouds and trying to avoid human society.

The classical Greeks were fascinated by the three-headed Chimera, a winged beast with the head of a lion, a goat, and a snake. In Greek tales, the Chimera breathes fire and has an appetite for human flesh.

Bellerophon hoped to capture Pegasus and make the horse his ally. But he had no idea how to go about doing that. Polyeidus therefore advised the young man to spend the night in one of the many Greek temples of the goddess of wisdom, Athena. There Bellerophon fell asleep, and in a dream the goddess appeared and told him how to capture the winged horse.

The next morning, the young man followed Athena's instructions, and soon he was riding Pegasus through the air on the way to find the lethal Chimera. The dragon-like monster was gnawing on a dead human body when the man and horse drew near. Immediately, the creature sensed the potential of another meal and leapt up into the air in hopes of snaring its prey. But riding atop the marvelous white stallion, Bellerophon was able to stay always above the Chimera and out of reach of its bloodstained claws. Eventually, the beast became exhausted from the chase and faltered. At that point Pegasus swooped downward, and the young man on its back hurled a spear down the Chimera's throat. The monster then fell to earth with a thud, and its fiery breath, now turned inward, burned it to ashes.

WORD ORIGINS

air

In modern life: the invisible gases that living things breathe in and out.

In ancient Greece: *aer*, the Greek word for "atmosphere."

The Hydra and Its Heads

To the classical Greeks, the story of the Chimera and its fiery breath was not just an old folktale designed to entertain people sitting at a hearth or campfire on a winter's night. Rather, the Greeks recognized various concepts and customs in the myth as reflections of their own world and customs. First, like other mythical Greek dragons, the Chimera itself had become an ill omen. The Greeks strongly believed in omens—natural signs of impending events, either good or bad. Dragons, especially the Chimera, were seen as omens that foretold future natural disasters.

In particular, fire-breathing dragons were associated with volcanoes and the red-hot gases and lava they spewed across the countryside. In fact, a volcano in Lycia, the very place the Chimera ravaged

The Brain Dragon

In his 2002 book, *An Instinct for Dragons*, anthropologist David E. Jones attempted to explain why the Greeks and some other ancient peoples strongly emphasized dragons in their myths. He argued that the ancestors of humans—tree-dwelling African primates—struggled to escape from three basic forms of predator: leopards and other big cats, pythons and other huge snakes, and eagles and similar hunting birds, or raptors. The dragon, Jones said, was a frightening image made up of a combination of traits from those major predators. In a summary of Jones's theory, Montana State University scholar Paul A. Trout writes:

> Ancient primates evolved alarm calls to identify each of the three predators, with each call triggering the defensive response appropriate to the nature of the attack mode of the specific predator. Jones calls this predator-recognition template the "snake/raptor/cat complex." This complex is the source of what Jones refers to as the "brain dragon." The brain dragon emerged when our apelike ancestors left the trees to walk on the ground. Rather suddenly, the relatively small brain of [early humans] had to process a lot of information about many new forms of predators and develop new alarm calls and strategic responses to them. Faced with information overload, [that brain] resorted to lumping information into manageable and memorable chunks. As a result, the cat, the snake, and the raptor were merged into a hybrid creature that had the salient predatory features of each, [a] "monster" that came to be known as the "dragon."

Paul A. Trout, "Why We Invented Monsters." *Salon*, December 3, 2011. www.salon.com.

in the myth, was so often active in classical times that it acquired the name Mount Chimera. The first-century-CE Roman scholar Pliny the Elder discussed the volcanoes of his day, including Mount Chimera. It "blazes day and night with a continuous flame," he wrote. Moreover, "even the stones and sand in [local] rivers glow." Supposedly, Pliny said, when people dug down into the ground in that region, "streams of fire follow."[20]

Roman intellectuals like Pliny and earlier Greek ones like Plato and Aristotle understood that dragons like the Chimera had never actually existed. Instead, they reasoned, ancient volcanic eruptions had given rise to the legends of fire-breathing creatures. However, an undetermined percentage of average, uneducated, and illiterate Greeks did accept that such monsters had once existed and might *still* exist in remote regions.

The issue of ancient belief in dragons aside, modern scholars see other parallels between Greek mythical dragons and ancient volcanic activity. A clear example is the myth of the Hydra. It had a big, slippery, snakelike body and nine dragonlike heads. According to legend, when someone sliced off one of its heads, one or two more quickly grew to replace it. This clearly made the monster extremely hard to destroy.

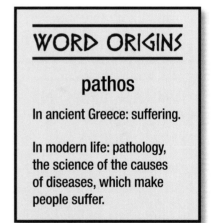

WORD ORIGINS

pathos

In ancient Greece: suffering.

In modern life: pathology, the science of the causes of diseases, which make people suffer.

In the Hydra's chief myth, it assaulted the area around Lerna in southeastern Greece, causing widespread pathos, or suffering. It lumbered from place to place, eating cattle, horses, and other animals and destroying farms and country houses. Finally, however, the famous strongman Heracles came along and fought and killed the beast. The ancient Greek writer Apollodorus of Athens described the battle. "Heracles went to Lerna," he wrote, and

found the Hydra on the brow of a hill [where the monster] had its den. Shooting at it with flaming arrows, Heracles drove the creature out, and then, when it came close, he grabbed it and held it tight. But the Hydra wrapped itself around his foot, and he was not able to get free by striking off its heads with his club, for as soon as one head was cut off, two grew in its place. [Eventually], by burning the stumps of the Hydra's heads with firebrands, [Heracles] kept them from growing out again.[21]

Some modern experts see the Hydra's heads as symbolic of volcanic lava tubes and vents. In some types of eruption, they point out, hot magma and gases travel through underground tubes and at unexpected times and places burst above ground, forming vents. At times a vent goes dormant as the hot materials change directions and burst through the surface nearby, creating one or more fresh vents. In very ancient times this sort of activity may have inspired the tale of new dragon's heads forming in place of lost ones.

The Colchian Dragon

Several other dragons mentioned in the Greek myths seem to have been based more on real animals than on natural forces or disasters. A good example was the so-called Colchian dragon, named for the land of Colchis. That region was located along the eastern shores of the Black Sea, which the early Greeks envisioned as a faraway, exotic place.

Colchis and its dragon figured prominently in the renowned Greek adventure tale often referred to as the Argonautica, meaning "Voyage of the *Argo*." The *Argo* was the ship that carried the famous Argonauts, led by the hero Jason, in search of the Golden Fleece, the hide of a magical ram. After a series of hair-raising exploits, the Argonauts reached Colchis, where, rumor had it, the local king kept the fleece.

> ## WORD ORIGINS
>
> ### *sauros*
>
> In ancient Greece: the word for "lizard."
>
> In modern life: dinosaur, one of many species of extinct lizard-like animals.

The rumor proved true, and Jason hastened to swipe the fleece and take it back to Greece. But he soon found that the fabulous relic was guarded by a fearsome creature that appeared to be a kind of lizard, which the Greeks called a *sauros*. Only this lizard was gigantic and possessed many large coils—long, snakelike body parts.

Heracles prepares to strike the Hydra, a monster with a snakelike body and nine dragon-like heads. Once Heracles realizes that cutting off the heads results in the growth of new heads, he resorts to fire to kill the beast.

In the telling of the myth by the third-century-BCE Greek poet Apollonius of Rhodes, Jason and his ally Medea saw that the fleece hung from an oak tree. A dragon carefully guarded the prize. "The serpent with his keen sleepless eyes saw them coming, and stretched out his long neck and hissed [at them]. The monster rolled his countless coils covered with hard dry scales." Then it "raised aloft his grisly head, eager to enclose them both in his murderous jaws."[22] Fortunately, however, Medea was skilled in the use of potent herbs and managed to drug the creature, which fell into a deep sleep. (In an alternate version of the myth, Jason fought and killed the dragon.) With the beast incapacitated, Jason was able to capture the fleece.

Myth-Tellers' Corner: Ovid

One of the most important ancient tellers of the Greek myths was a Roman poet named Publius Ovidius Naso, who lived from 43 BCE until 17 CE. In his own time and ever after, he was better known by his nickname—Ovid. Much of the great popularity he enjoyed stemmed from his lighthearted, usually witty poems about love. Some of them also made fairly graphic references to sex, which bothered more conservative Romans, including the then ruling first emperor, Augustus. A prudish individual, Augustus eventually grew irritated with Ovid and in 8 CE exiled him to a drab frontier town on the shores of the Black Sea. The poet died there nine years later.

Ovid's substantial output of literary works also included a large-scale collection of Greek myths, the *Metamorphoses.* One of his major modern translators, Mary M. Innes, states that he

> infused new life into the old stories, retelling them with the inimitable [matchless] grace and practiced ease of one who knows well how to hold his audience. The result is a treasure-house of myth and legend which was read with delight in his own day, and has continued to charm succeeding generations, providing a source from which the whole of Western European literature has derived inspiration.

Indeed, Ovid became the most popular Roman poet of the European Renaissance (circa 1350 to 1600). His compendium of myths strongly influenced later writers as well, among them the great English playwright William Shakespeare.

Mary M. Innes, introduction to Ovid, *Metamorphoses,* trans. Mary M. Innes. New York: Penguin, 2006, p. 9.

Ladon and Cetus

The Colchian dragon was in good company, so to speak. The concept of a dragon or other reptilian monster guarding a valuable object or treasure was very common in Greek mythology. Another prominent example was Ladon, a hundred-headed dragon that watched over the golden apples of the Hesperides, daughters of the Titan Atlas. Ladon met its doom at the hands of the same hero who had slain the Hydra—the mighty Heracles. Afterward, the leader of the Olympian gods, Zeus, placed Ladon in the *polos*, or sky, where it rested ever after as the constellation Draco (the dragon).

Heracles himself, under his Roman name, Hercules, also became a star group, situated right beside the constellation of the monster he had killed. An unknown third-century-CE Greek or Roman author that modern experts call Pseudo-Hyginus described these ancient constellations. Hercules was visible above Draco, he wrote, and the hero was "prepared to fight, with his left hand holding his lion skin, and his right the club. He is trying to kill the dragon of the Hesperides, which, it is thought, never was overcome by sleep or closed its eyes, thus offering more proof it was placed there as a guard. [Hercules] appears to be fighting with all his strength."[23]

Still another mythical Greek dragon—the sea monster Cetus—also ended up as a constellation in the night sky. In that widely retold tale, the sea god Poseidon sent Cetus to devastate the land of Ethiopia to punish its queen for making a remark he deemed offensive. The hero Perseus bravely slew the huge creature. According to the first-century-BCE Roman myth-teller Ovid, Perseus

suddenly sprang from the ground and soared into the clouds. The dragon saw his shadow on the sea and savaged [clawed at] what it saw, [after which] Perseus, swooping headlong through the void, attacked the monster's back and, as it roared, deep in its shoulder sank his crescent blade. Wounded so sorely, the beast now reared upright, high in the air, now dived below the waves, now turned like a fierce boar in frenzy when the pack [of hunting dogs] bays all around. On his swift wings Perseus eluded the snapping fangs and struck the parts exposed and plunged his curved sword between its ribs and in its back, all rough with barnacles, and where its tapering tail ended in a fish. The beast belched purple blood, sea spume and blood together.[24]

Avid Stargazers

Long afterward, a god placed both Perseus and Cetus in the starry heavens. These constellations depicting dragons and the heroes who killed them were very meaningful to the classical Greeks, who were avid stargazers. On the one hand, they used the stars to navigate on both sea and land. On the other, like most other ancient people, the Greeks held that the movements of the stars and planets affected the lives of people on earth—a belief system known both then and now as astrology. It began in Babylonia, in what is now Iraq, no later than the mid-second millennium BCE. At that time Greece was still in its Bronze Age. Much later, in the 200s BCE, astrology began to catch on in Greece, and by the first century BCE large numbers of Greeks employed horoscopes. They hoped these would show whether they would encounter good or bad fortune in the future.

The dragon constellations played a potentially potent role in such predictions. For instance, if a person was born when a comet appeared within the boundaries of one of those sky monsters, he or she could expect to be plagued by bad luck. Some people took such forecasts quite seriously, constituting one of the many ways, big and small, that myths affected the daily lives of the ancient Greeks.

Chapter Four

Sinister Creatures with Women's Faces

Even a brief survey of the ancient Greek monster myths reveals an intriguing thematic pattern. Namely, the ancient myth-tellers described an unusually large proportion of these creatures either as female or as possessing a woman's face. The reasons for this phenomenon are not completely clear. However, most modern experts think it was partly due to the fact that as a rule, Greek men viewed women as socially and even naturally inferior. Indeed, most men saw members of the other gender as less intelligent than men. A fair percentage of men went further, moreover, viewing women in general as not very trustworthy, at times mystifying, frustrating to deal with, and in some cases even dangerous to men.

That such attitudes toward women existed can clearly be seen in surviving remarks by male Greek writers. Several of those men justified their belief in female inferiority by citing the well-known myth of the supposed first woman, Pandora. The god Prometheus, the story went, created her from mud. Not long afterward, she opened a special box she was told not to touch and in so doing released misery, hatred, greed, and all the other ills that have plagued humanity ever since.

The epic poet Hesiod was only one of many Greek men who felt that the events of that myth really happened and had tainted all future women. From her, Hesiod, said, "is the race of women and female kind. Of her is the deadly race and tribe of women who live amongst mortal men to their great trouble, no helpmates in hateful poverty, but only in wealth."[25] This and other remarks Hesiod made show he was unhappily married and viewed his wife as a shallow, scheming person who cared more about money than him.

Certainly not all Greek men were as extreme in their distrust in and scorn for women as Hesiod was. Yet there is no doubt that classical Greek society was highly paternal, or male dominated, a system widely viewed as justified by Pandora's story. "In depicting women

Ignoring warnings from the gods, Pandora opens the box that releases misery, hatred, greed, and other ills into the world. Stories like this one illustrate the negative views toward women that permeated segments of ancient Greek society.

as untrustworthy and even devious," researcher Sabine McKellen writes, the Pandora myth "supports the paternal structure of ancient Greek culture." Women's "legal and citizenship status," she continues, was

> largely regulated by, and subordinate to, men. This particular origin story underscores the realities of ancient Athenian society, where women had no independent legal status. A woman was forever under some form of guardianship—first that of her father or another male relative, then that of her husband. With men overseeing the economic aspects of her life, an ancient Athenian woman also was banned from public life and unable to own property.[26]

The Sphinx and Her Riddle

It appears likely that the earliest Greek myth-tellers saw most women as Hesiod did—as untrustworthy creatures responsible for much of the misery that afflicted society. This attitude comes through strongly in the famous tale of the Sphinx that terrorized the Greek city of Thebes, located in the Greek mainland's south-central region. The female creature, based on an Egyptian mythical beast, was another of the many composite monsters in Greek mythology. According to one ancient myth-teller, "She had a woman's face, the breast, feet, and tail of a lion, and bird's wings."[27]

One by one, the Sphinx cornered Thebans outside the city, tore them apart, and devoured them. However, before killing them she first posed a riddle to each. The first-century-CE Greek writer now called Pseudo-Apollodorus explained, "The riddle was: what is it that has one voice, and is four-footed and two-footed and three-footed?" A priestess had told the Thebans that "they would be free of the Sphinx when they guessed her riddle, so they often [got together] to search for the meaning." Unfortunately for them, however, "whenever they came up with the wrong answer, she would seize one of them, and eat him up."[28]

Many months went by and the Thebans still saw no way out of their awful dilemma. But then, seemingly out of nowhere, a *xenos*, or stranger, appeared—a strong, strapping young man. He said his name was Oedipus and that he was a native of Corinth, a city situated several miles southwest of Thebes. Oedipus also said that he was not afraid of the Sphinx and to everyone's surprise marched out of the city and confronted the monster.

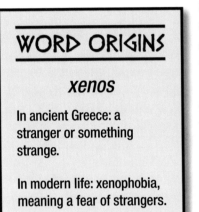

WORD ORIGINS

xenos

In ancient Greece: a stranger or something strange.

In modern life: xenophobia, meaning a fear of strangers.

Evidently thinking the man would soon be her next meal, the repulsive creature confidently posed her signature riddle. But to her utter surprise, Oedipus knew the right answer. The living thing that starts out four footed, then becomes two footed, and ends up three footed, he said, is a human being. As a baby he crawls on all fours, as an adult he walks on two feet, and as an old man he uses a cane—in a sense a third foot.

It was clear that the Sphinx felt both humiliated and defeated at being outwitted. Worse still, she no longer desired to go on living. Some ancient writers said she produced a sword and plunged it into her own heart, whereas others, including Pseudo-Apollodorus, claimed she jumped off a tall building or cliff and died from the fall. Whatever the means of the Sphinx's demise, the Thebans were overjoyed and repaid Oedipus's brave feat by making him king of their city.

The story of the Sphinx was one of the most popular myths perpetuated by the classical Greeks. Perhaps because of her association with riddles, she became a symbol of mystery. Indeed, the Greeks thoroughly enjoyed inventing and posing riddles, just as the Sphinx had done in the myth. Moreover, it was thought that when the gods communicated with people, they often did so in riddles. At the Temple of Apollo at Delphi (in central Greece), for example, priestesses called oracles conveyed the supposed words of that deity to religious pilgrims. Those divine responses were almost always couched in the form of riddles. The Greeks also portrayed the Sphinx in art, especially sculptures placed inside or outside of tombs. These were usually painted in bright colors.

Oedipus confronts the Sphinx, a monster with the face of a woman and the breast, feet, and tail of a lion. The bones of those who tried and failed to answer her riddles lie at the base of her lair.

Too Lethal to Look At

Even more frightening and famous than the Sphinx in Greek mythology was another monster with a woman's face—the Gorgon Medusa. Her main claim to fame was her ability to kill someone using only her bloodcurdling gaze. Ovid described large numbers of lifelike statues of humans and animals who had had the misfortune to look directly at Medusa. "The sight of the Gorgon," he said, "had changed them from their true selves"[29] into *lithos*, or solid stone.

There were various ancient accounts of where the ghastly Gorgons dwelled. Hesiod claimed they lived "beyond the stream of the famous Ocean, on the [world's] edge near night."[30] Other myth-tellers said Medusa and her other hideous sisters inhabited a remote, little-known island, and still others placed them in the wilderness of faraway Libya, in North Africa.

One of the more unexpected elements of Medusa's myth was the fact that she had started out not as a monster but as a beautiful young woman. Her mistake was to agree to make love to the sea god Poseidon inside a temple dedicated to his divine sister, the war goddess Athena. To punish Medusa for defiling the temple, the angry Athena transformed her into the hideous creature that thereafter was too lethal to look at.

Medusa continued to turn people into stone pillars until she finally met her match in a courageous young man named Perseus. Fortunately for him, he did not undertake his mission to destroy her alone. First, he gained the aid of the messenger god, Hermes, who guided him to the Gorgons' secluded island. Hermes also gave him a pair of winged sandals that allowed him to fly and a cap that made him invisible when he wore it. Another deity who helped Perseus was Athena, who still held a grudge against Medusa. Exercising her talents as goddess of *sophia*, or wisdom, Athena presented Perseus with a highly polished metal shield that she said would keep him safe from the monster's deadly gaze.

Armed with these gifts, Perseus flew to the island. He saw the seemingly countless statues of humans and animals that had once held the breath of life and pitied them. Then he located the monster who had slain them—Medusa—who was asleep on a large, flat rock. As Athena had instructed him, he did not stare directly at Medusa's face. Instead, he looked only at her harmless reflection in the shield's shiny surface.

Myth-Tellers' Corner: Pseudo-Apollodorus

Some modern experts have called a text titled the *Bibliotheca* (library) the single most valuable ancient work on mythology that has survived to the present. For centuries it was attributed to a Greek writer and myth-teller named Apollodorus of Athens. But various clues were eventually found showing that someone else wrote it. The identity of that individual, who may have lived in the first century CE or somewhat later, remains unknown. So scholars have come to call him Pseudo-Apollodorus (or false Apollodorus). Unfortunately for modern observers who admire his work, nothing for certain is known about his life.

The *Bibliotheca* is divided into three overall sections labeled "books." The first book covers the creation of the cosmos and the early gods and natural forces involved in it, the origins of the Olympian gods, the exploits of several early Greek kings, and the Argonautica. The second book includes the adventures of Bellerophon, Perseus, Heracles, and other heroes who slew monsters. Finally, the third book recounts the myths of early Crete, the founding of Thebes, the story of Oedipus, and the exploits of the Athenian hero Theseus.

The work's third book is incomplete, however. Remarks by certain ancient writers indicate that Pseudo-Apollodorus originally included a detailed telling of the Trojan War. Somehow that section was lost over the centuries. But the fact that most of the work has survived has been a boon to modern historians and other scholars, along with everyone else who enjoys the ancient Greek myths.

Through that mirror image, Perseus watched the demon-like creature awaken. It was plain that, though he was invisible to her, she could smell him or otherwise sense his presence because she scanned the area intently as if looking for intruders. Hovering not far above her, he waited for just the right moment and then dove downward, his sword arm raised. In a single, deliberate motion, he swung the weapon and separated her snake-infested head from her body, which sprayed blood all over as it fell lifeless onto the rock. The young man then collected her hideous head in a sack and flew away.

As he went, Perseus glanced back just long enough see something unexpected and wondrous occur. Out of the Gorgon's blood-soaked corpse crawled two magnificent beings. One was the winged horse that would come to be known as Pegasus. The other was a tall, handsome, human-looking warrior—Chrysoar, the son of Medusa.

A Sense of Artistic Struggle

Evidence suggests that to the classical Greeks Medusa was one of the most popular, if not *the* most popular, of the mythical monsters. This made her tale not only a favorite of storytellers, but also a major inspiration for artists. Yet depicting her was no easy task. Indeed, she was purportedly so evil and unsightly that capturing her image in art in a realistic manner often proved extremely challenging. "Monsters in general," the late, great scholar C.M. Bowra pointed out,

> depend for their horror on being vague and dimly conceived and are usually ineffective in any art form that insists on making them realistic. Such a creature as the Gorgon Medusa, which was believed to turn men into stone by its mere look, can never be adequately portrayed by human hands, and though Greek Gorgons indeed make ugly grimaces [in paintings and sculptures], they hardly freeze the blood.[31]

This difficulty in portraying such monsters as truly frightening frequently prompted Greek artists to cheat a little by making changes in the original myths. Historian Charles Freeman cites the example of a sculpture of Medusa created circa 600 BCE for the western porch of the Temple of Artemis on the Greek island of Corfu. "Medusa is shown with her head on," he explains,

> but also with her two offspring, the winged horse Pegasus and her son, [the warrior] Chrysoar. In the myth, these two were only born at the moment she was decapitated by Perseus. In

other words, a story incompatible with the original myth has to be created in order to preserve Medusa in her full power alongside her children. Again, the problems of narrative have defeated the artist. [There] is a real sense of artistic struggle, a feeling that the artist knows what he wants to do but is restricted.

The ultimate lesson the classical Greeks learned, Freeman adds, was that "their favorite stories could not be translated easily into art."[32]

Greek artists had similar difficulty in creating suitably scary versions of another monster with a woman's face—the harpy. Harpies were hideous, birdlike beasts with wings and sharp claws. A common nickname for them in the Greek myths was "snatchers," based on their

Flying Argonauts chase away two harpies that have been stealing human food. According to Greek myths, a harpy is a hideous creature with wings, sharp claws, and a head that is part woman and part bird.

Seeking Medusa's Protection

The classical Greeks portrayed the terrifying head of the Gorgon Medusa so often in paintings, sculptures, and other artistic mediums that they developed a special word for such a work—*gorgoneion*. A good example is a surviving sculpted *gorgoneion* from the Temple of Artemis on the island of Corcyra (along Greece's western coast). The stone relic once rested above one of the temple's column-lined porches. The artist gave Medusa a round, broad face with a twisted grin and grotesque, bulging eyes. Other classical Greek artists gave her masculine-looking beards, ugly snub noses, big tusks, creepy-looking tongues protruding from the mouth, scaly skin, and birdlike claws and wings.

One important reason the Greeks chose to adorn the exteriors of temples with Medusa's image was that people thought it could ward off evil. "In the Greco-Roman world," researcher John Mancini explains, the *gorgoneion* "was a protective amulet, similar to the 'evil eye' of witchcraft." The potent power it supposedly held "could be transferred to whoever possessed it." Therefore, people also placed images of Medusa and her sister Gorgons on their front doors and on the insides or outsides of their tombs. In addition, Mancini continues, many Greek soldiers "desired the deadly effects or protection of the Gorgon. Indeed, some of the earliest depictions of the gorgoneion in Greece appear on the shields of warriors in the mid-fifth century BCE, where she is represented as a goat-bearded monster with tusks."

John Mancini, "Pursuing the Gorgon Medusa," *Classical Wisdom Weekly,* July 16, 2014. http://classical wisdom.com.

habit of stealing food from people just as they were about to eat. The creatures also sometimes squirted their disgusting bodily fluids onto people's meals, rendering them inedible. One of the more famous tales featuring harpies was the Argonautica. While searching for the

Golden Fleece, Jason and his men found an old man who was starving because harpies kept taking his food, and the men proceeded to rescue him from his dilemma.

The Old Hags in the Mirror

Particularly difficult for the Greeks to portray in art was Akhlys, the female spirit of misery, sadness, and death. In his work *Shield of Heracles*, Hesiod described her as "mournful and fearful, pale, shriveled, shrunk with hunger, swollen-kneed. Long nails tipped her hands, and she dribbled at the nose, and from her cheeks blood dripped down to the ground. She stood leering hideously, and much dust, sodden with tears, lay upon her shoulders."[33]

Akhlys was the incarnation, or living form, of the clouding over of a person's eyes in the seconds following death. In that form she appeared indirectly, most often unnamed, in the numerous myths in which human characters died. In the hands of classical Greek artists, hers was one of the first ancient portrayals of a stereotypical character present in most past societies and even a few present ones—the old hag or female witch.

The best-known ancient Greek sculpture that captured that character is today known as the *Drunk Old Woman*, which dates from the late third century BCE. That the statue was mainly intended to portray an aged, poverty-stricken, alcoholic woman was no accident. Both before and during classical times, myth-tellers who described and perpetuated Akhlys's image undoubtedly used dirt-poor, worn-out old women in their own midst as models for her.

WORD ORIGINS

aristos

In ancient Greece: best.

In modern life: aristocrat, meaning someone belonging to the best social class or best families.

That such sad cases still existed in classical times is a powerful reminder that Greek society in that era was not as idyllic as some modern writers and artists have described it. It is not uncommon today for books about ancient Greece to focus mainly on its *aristos*, or best, qualities and achievements. Typically these include the fit, muscular Olympic athletes; the insightful philosophers and scientists; and the brilliant playwrights, democratic reformers, and artists of Greece's so-called cultural golden age.

Frequently left out of such generalized, sanitized portrayals is the extreme poverty that always existed among Greek society's lowest classes. The most destitute among the poor were quite often the grossly overworked wives, mothers, and grandmothers. Often as they aged they grew increasingly haggard from a demoralizing combination of multiple pregnancies, relentless physical labor, disease, and lack of effective health care. Although it was horribly unfair and unjust, society continued to use the worst off of those unfortunate women as, in a sense, mirrors. It was their reflections that supplied most Greeks with visual images for the death hags, harpies, witches, and several other female monsters from the age-old myths.

Chapter Five

Mythical Monsters in Modern Culture

Although the renowned civilization created by the classical Greeks perished long ago, numerous aspects of what they called their *paedeia*, or culture—survive today. Indeed, the democratic ideas, theatrical inventions, philosophical concepts, literary inventions, and other elements of the Greek achievement went on to form much of the basic foundation of Western civilization. (That term generally refers to the society that developed in Europe after the end of ancient times and later in the Americas and other lands colonized by Europeans.)

Part of that splendid cultural heritage the Greeks bequeathed to later generations was Greece's large treasury of myths. Many of the old tales of gods, goddesses, human heroes, and their accomplishments, adventures, and interactions remain recognizable to and popular among millions of people today. Especially popular are the monsters populating those myths, including huge primeval beasts, giants, serpents, dragons, and hideous creatures like Medusa and the harpies. In part, their fame is due to their enduring power to entertain. As was the case in past generations, today both children and adults continue to harbor a fascination for strange and scary creatures that threaten to destroy the normal order of things.

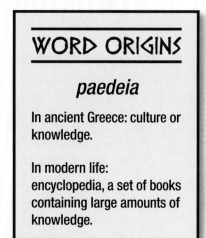

WORD ORIGINS

paedeia

In ancient Greece: culture or knowledge.

In modern life: encyclopedia, a set of books containing large amounts of knowledge.

Also, states science writer Matt Kaplan, "monsters may be serving a valuable purpose in society." By standing in for people's main fears,

> and allowing these to be discussed and explored in a safe environment, monsters might be making it feasible for these fears to be more effectively prepared for and ultimately faced. So the benefits of being a courageous individual can be more readily reaped. Like lion cubs play-fighting in the safety of their den, monsters may be allowing threats to be toyed with in the safe sandbox of the imagination.[34]

For these and perhaps other reasons, the monsters from the Greek myths have invaded every possible niche of the many modern artistic and entertainment media. Only a partial list includes paintings, sculptures, novels, plays, music, television shows, movies, comic books, and video games. As a result, these ancient creatures have become, in a sense, interwoven threads of the West's complex cultural cloth.

A Long Process of Survival

Although the Greek city-states and kingdoms did not survive, their rich collection of myths lived on. Beginning in the second century BCE the Romans conquered and absorbed most of the Greek lands, which were never again independent nations. (No single country of Greece existed until the emergence of the modern Greek nation in 1830.) Yet fortunately for the Greeks, the Romans were both fascinated and awed by Greek culture. So they eagerly adopted and perpetuated it, along with its myths, in the process melding the two societies into what became known as Greco-Roman, or classical, civilization. During the roughly six centuries that followed, therefore, the Greek myths were in no danger of being lost to humanity.

The first major threat to those stories' survival came when the Roman Empire disintegrated in the late 400s and early 500s CE. The formal, large-scale societal apparatus that passed Greco-Roman culture from one generation to another was gone. However, once again Greek culture was fortunate. In a totally unexpected development, Christian churchmen filled the void left by Greco-Roman society's collapse. Medieval Christian thinkers, writers, and monks felt that the ancient myths were useful for various purposes. One appealed to their vanity, as they found that quoting from the old myths gave their own writings and lectures a more educated, learned look.

Churchmen also kept the myths alive by copying and recopying some of the large-scale Greco-Roman compilations of myths. One of the more popular was Ovid's *Metamorphoses*. Monks often took his versions of the old stories and rewrote them a bit in order to make moral points to their Christian flocks.

This process kept most of the old myths, including those featuring dragons, one-eyed giants, and creepy harpies, alive long enough for the artists of the Renaissance to discover them. The last phase of the medieval era, the Renaissance (circa 1300 to 1600), witnessed a major outburst of European literary and artistic creation. During this period writers, painters, sculptors, and other innovative people incorporated Greek mythical characters, several monsters among them, into their works. This had the effect of widening their appeal and permanently embedding them in the West's growing collection of fine arts.

Sky Maps, Paintings, and Sculptures

One of the more striking mythology-inspired works produced during the Renaissance featured several different Greek mythical monsters. Called the *Sky-Map of the Northern Hemisphere*, it was completed in 1515 by German artist Albrecht Dürer. It consists of a large circle, or *kuklos*, containing dozens of star groups from the night sky. Among the mythical images that are each represented by an *astron*, or constellation, are Perseus holding Medusa's decapitated head, that hero's famous steed Pegasus, the dragon-like Hydra, and the mighty Heracles swinging his club at another dragon, Ladon (in the form of the constellation Draco).

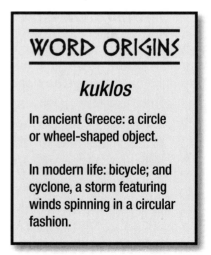

WORD ORIGINS

kuklos

In ancient Greece: a circle or wheel-shaped object.

In modern life: bicycle; and cyclone, a storm featuring winds spinning in a circular fashion.

The Renaissance was also known for its many talented painters, some of whom committed Greek monsters to their canvases. The renowned Italian artist Leonardo da Vinci was one. His oil painting of the head of the Gorgon Medusa, of uncertain date, remains legendary, although the work itself was subsequently lost. The most famous surviving painting of Medusa was created by another Renaissance painter, Caravaggio. It inspired pictures of her by later leading artists, including Peter Paul Rubens.

Sculptors, both during and after the Renaissance, also produced versions of the Greeks' favorite mythical monster, Medusa. Of these works, by far the best known and influential is the one by Italy's Benvenuto Cellini. His masterwork, depicting both Perseus and Medusa, is made of bronze and stands 18 feet (5.5 m) tall. The hero grasps his sword in his right hand, while his left hand holds the recently slain Gorgon's snake-haired head. Medusa's lifeless body sprawls at her killer's feet. Another well-known version of the same scene, carved from marble, was fashioned in 1801 by noted Italian sculptor Antonio Canova.

Monster Myths and History

Another way that the monsters of the Greek myths were perpetuated in Western society was through studies of them by archaeologists and other scholars who popularized their findings and theories in books. In many cases these experts found evidence suggesting that certain myths about monsters were based on real historical events or realities. One example involves the renowned Minotaur—the flesh-eating bull-man who dwelled in the Cretan maze known as the Labyrinth. Some of the evidence in question indicates that in Bronze Age Minoan society both priestesses and priests performed dances, sacrifices, and other sacred rites. Moreover, it appears that they frequently wore bull masks while doing so. Some scholars suspect that during Greece's later Dark Age, garbled cultural memories of those masked Minoan clergy inspired the legend of the Minotaur, with its humanlike body and bull's head.

The seventeenth-century Flemish painter Peter Paul Rubens created a haunting image of the severed head of Medusa (pictured). Hideous creatures from Greek mythology still fascinate readers, moviegoers, and art lovers.

Similarly, recent discoveries suggest that the ancient Greek tales of the strange beaked creatures called griffins were also based in fact. Among the evidence the Greeks themselves cited for the existence of griffins consisted of odd-looking skeletons found in the region of Scythia, north of Greece. In the early twentieth century, scientists began digging up identical skeletons in the same region. But these modern excavators were armed with something the ancients lacked—namely, knowledge of dinosaurs. Those bones belonged to a small beaked dinosaur the experts dubbed protoceratops. The Greeks did not realize the skeletons were millions of years old, so they assumed they belonged to a strange, still living beast they came to call the griffin.

Among the other historical events on which some Greek monster myths seem to have been based were large-scale natural disasters. For example, some experts contend that the episode with the bronze giant Talos in the Argonautica is a mangled memory of a real volcanic event. Talos supposedly hurled huge rocks at approaching ships, including Jason's *Argo*. Scientists have shown conclusively that circa 1650 BCE, during the Bronze Age, the volcano on the small island of Thera

Fossils discovered by the ancient Greeks supported their belief in the existence of strange beaked creatures called griffins. In more recent times these fossils have been identified as belonging to a dinosaur known as protoceratops (pictured).

(today called Santorini), situated north of Crete, erupted violently. Moreover, during the eruption huge boulders were thrown outward for many miles. Those volcanic missiles would have made a powerful impression on any sailors who witnessed the eruption from a distance, and their accounts might later have been incorporated into the evolving myth of Jason and the Argonauts.

This same mythmaking process has also sometimes worked in reverse. That is, instead of a Greek monster myth arising from an event in an *earlier* era, in some instances such monster tales themselves gave rise to new monster tales in *later* ages. The most often cited example is the widely famous medieval Christian myth of Saint George slaying a dragon. A number of modern scholars suggest that that medieval tale was based directly on the Greek myth of Bellerophon's fight with the dragon-like Chimera.

The process of basing later stories, along with new artistic and cultural works, on the ancient monster myths extended in various ways into the twentieth century. For instance, numerous modern novels and songs have reinterpreted and retold the tales of Medusa, the Minotaur, the Chimera, and other legendary Greek monsters. Two such young adult novels—Rick Riordan's *The Sea of Monsters* (2006) and *The Battle of the Labyrinth* (2008)—were best sellers. As for songs, in 2008 the American heavy metal band Trivium released its tune "Torn Between Scylla and Charybdis," about two giant ancient Greek monsters that regularly threatened sailors; similarly, the popular American rock band Smashing Pumpkins introduced the song "Chimera" in 2012.

The Dragon and the Whirlpool

Trivium's 2008 song "Torn Between Scylla and Charybdis" was based on two of the most frightening of all the Greek mythical monsters. These deadly creatures were said to dwell on the opposite shores of the Strait of Messina, which separates Italy's southern mainland from the large island of Sicily. According to one ancient myth, Scylla started out as a beautiful young nature goddess. She fell in love with the ruler of the seas, Poseidon, which caused his wife, Amphitrite, to grow fiercely jealous. Amphitrite punished Scylla by transforming her into a six-headed dragon-like monster that tried to snatch sailors from their ships when they passed near her shore. Charybdis also began as a lovely young nature goddess. Zeus, leader of the gods, turned her into a giant whirlpool that sucked in vessels that ventured into the strait. In Homer's famous epic poem, the *Odyssey,* the chief character, Odysseus, is almost swallowed up by Charybdis and barely survives by grabbing hold of a tree limb overhanging the great whirlpool. The ancient stories about the two monsters gave rise to the expression "caught between Scylla and Charybdis," meaning having to choose between two equally unpleasant choices.

Mythical Monsters in Movies

By far the most widely popular and influential modern art form—the motion picture—has also frequently tackled the Greek mythical monsters. Innumerable movies—both silent and sound—have featured one or more of those colorful creatures. One such monster that has been unusually popular among filmmakers is the Minotaur. The sound films alone in which it appears number at least twenty-three.

One notable example was *Minotaur*, released in 2006. Set in Bronze Age Greece, it follows a hero named Theo (clearly based on Theseus) who kills a bull-monster that has been terrorizing his village. The 2001 film *Immortals* also takes place in ancient times. It involves a man in a bull mask who does the villain's dirty work until a hero comes along and slays that henchman in a maze (corresponding to the Labyrinth in the original myth).

Several of the most famous ancient Greek monsters appear in one of the finest movies ever made about Greek mythology—*Jason and the Argonauts* (1963). A retelling of parts of the Argonautica, it shows the harpies stealing food from an old man the Argonauts encounter on their way to Colchis. The film also includes Jason's fight with the Colchian dragon and the Argonauts' run-in with the bronze giant Talos.

These creatures were brilliantly brought to life on the screen by the late special effects wizard Ray Harryhausen (1920–2013). He was long the film industry's leading expert in stop-motion animation. Now largely replaced by digital animation, that process employs highly realistic-looking miniature models that are moved and photographed one frame at a time. When a projector plays back the film at normal speed (twenty-four frames per second), the model appears to live, breathe, and move.

Harryhausen also animated the Gorgon Medusa in the 1979 version of *Clash of the Titans* (which was remade in 2010). Here, he gave the monster a long, scaly tail instead of legs to make her look more alien and scary. Speaking about Harryhausen, historian Jon Solomon, an expert on movies about ancient history and mythology, praised "the superiority of his fantasy creations." His "genius takes our impression of the Greek mythological world into a new dimension of visual reality."[35]

Stop-motion animation legend Ray Harryhausen created a frighteningly realistic Hydra, pictured here fighting Jason in the 1963 movie Jason and the Argonauts. *Harryhausen also worked his magic to create a terrifying Medusa and many other monsters from Greek mythology.*

The Illusion of a Giant

Harryhausen's modeling and animation were particularly effective in making non-humanoid monsters come to life. But when depicting human-looking mythical creatures like giants, most filmmakers have instead cast living actors to play those characters. This approach calls for employing different kinds of visual special effects.

Such effects can be seen in the various film versions of Homer's *Odyssey*. Two of the best known are *Ulysses* (the Roman name for the character Odysseus), released in 1954, with Kirk Douglas in the title role; and a lavish 1997 TV miniseries, *The Odyssey*, starring Armand Assante as Odysseus. Both productions included the famous scene in which Odysseus and his men encounter the giant Cyclops Polyphemus.

Constructing and Animating Medusa

Many mythical creatures in movies have been created by putting actors in monster suits, which almost always made them look less than credible. The great Hollywood special effects expert Ray Harryhausen hated that approach and chose instead to animate his monsters using the seemingly magical process of stop-motion animation. His rendition of the Greek monster Medusa for the 1979 film *Clash of the Titans* was typical of his work. He began by constructing a model with a metal skeleton featuring movable miniature joints called armatures. There were individual armatures for Medusa's fingers, wrists, elbows, shoulders, and waist, and several more in the snakelike tail. When the skeleton was complete, layers of latex rubber molded to look like skin were added, along with scales, hair, wrinkles, and other details. The last step was to carefully paint the model, thereby adding natural coloring and still more detail.

When the model was complete, Harryhausen placed it on a realistic miniature set resting on a tabletop with his camera set up in front of it. Moving the Medusa model into a predetermined starting position, he snapped a single frame of film. Then he moved some of the model's body parts slightly, took another frame, moved them again, snapped still another frame, and continued to repeat that process. When played on a projector, the resulting footage made the Medusa model appear to move its hands, arms, head, tail, and even its eyes in a realistic manner.

The trick in making the giant look convincing was to create the illusion that the actor portraying him towered over the men playing the Greeks. One of the several kinds of mechanical and photographic effects involved in the 1954 film consisted of using oversized props. For example, the prop department fashioned a giant club. When the actors playing the Greeks stood next to the club and other oversized objects on the set, it gave the impression they were in a giant's lair.

Another kind of mechanical effect employed in the 1954 version of the myth is known as forced perspective. In the initial step, the camera operator placed the actor playing the Cyclops on one side of the frame (the rectangular picture one sees on the screen). Then he positioned the men portraying the Greeks on the other side of the frame, only standing considerably more distant from the camera than the giant. This created the illusion that Greeks were much smaller than Polyphemus.

The 1997 version of the myth used a more advanced special effects technique known as computer-generated imagery, or CGI. The object of this approach is to combine two separately photographed images in such a way that they appear as one. First, the crew filmed the actor portraying the giant standing on a set that was dressed to look like the inside of the Cyclops's cave. The actor was instructed to gaze downward at the empty floor near his feet while speaking his lines. Then a technician scanned this image into a computer. He also scanned in a separate image of the actors playing the Greeks, in their case looking upward while speaking their dialogue. Employing advanced computer software, the technician then combined the two digital images, creating the false impression that a giant was standing beside men a fraction of his size.

These films about giants and other Greek mythical monsters are invariably spectacular and cost millions of dollars to make, which reveals an important reality of modern Western culture. The producers of those movies would not raise and spend such immense sums if the monsters portrayed in them were not already fairly well known to and popular with the public at large. Such filmmakers know that over the centuries those scary but strongly compelling creatures became part of Western society's fabric. It has also become clear that of all the existing art forms, film is the most complex and thereby most capable of bringing those ancient tales to life. As Solomon aptly points out, movies continue to help make "these vivid legends of ancient Greece popular enough to live on two millennia after the peoples that fostered them have perished."[36]

Source Notes

Introduction: Monsters Reflected in a Distorting Mirror

1. Quoted in Alastair Sooke, "The Fantastical Beasts of Ancient Greece," BBC, January 13, 2015. www.bbc.com.

2. Edith Hamilton, *Mythology*. New York: Grand Central, 2011, p. 13.

3. John Camp and Elizabeth Fisher, *The World of the Ancient Greeks*. London: Thames and Hudson, 2002, p. 52.

4. Camp and Fisher, *The World of the Ancient Greeks*, pp. 61–62.

5. Quoted in Sooke, "The Fantastical Beasts of Ancient Greece."

Chapter One: Monsters from When the World Was New

6. Sarah B. Pomeroy et al., *Ancient Greece: A Political, Social, and Cultural History*. New York: Oxford University Press, 2007, p. 258.

7. Pseudo-Apollodorus, *Bibliotheca*, trans. Keith Aldrich, excerpted in Theoi Greek Mythology, "Typhoeus 1." www.theoi.com.

8. Hesiod, *Theogony*, in *Hesiod, The Homeric Hymns, and Homerica*, trans. H.G. Evelyn-White. Cambridge, MA: Harvard University Press, 1964, p. 135.

9. Philostratus, *Life of Apollonius of Tyana*, trans. Frederick C. Conybeare, excerpted in Theoi Greek Mythology, "Grypes." www.theoi.com.

10. Plato, *Phaedo*, in *The Dialogues of Plato*, trans. Benjamin Jowett. Chicago: Encyclopedia Britannica, 1952, p. 231.

Chapter Two: The Brutish Cyclopes and Other Giants

11. Charles Freeman, *The Greek Achievement*. New York: Viking, 1999, p. 81.

12. Virgil, *Aeneid*, trans. Cecil Day-Lewis, excerpted in Theoi Greek Mythology, "Cyclopes." www.theoi.com.

13. Pausanias, *Guide to Greece*, vol. 1, trans. Peter Levi. New York: Penguin, 1971, p. 191.

14. Homer, *Odyssey*, trans. E.V. Rieu. Baltimore, MD: Penguin, 1967, p. 142.

15. Frank Redmond, "The Concept of Civilization in Homer's *Odyssey*," Lucian of Samosata Project, 2011. https://lucianofsamosata .info.

16. Redmond, "The Concept of Civilization in Homer's *Odyssey*."

17. Virgil, *Aeneid*, excerpted in Theoi Greek Mythology, "Orion." www.theoi.com.

Chapter Three: Repulsive Reptilians Menace Society

18. Carl Sagan, *The Dragons of Eden*. New York: Ballantine, 1977, pp. 150–51.

19. Hesiod, *Theogony*, trans. H.G. Evelyn-White, p. 103.

20. Pliny the Elder, *Natural History*, excerpted in *Pliny the Elder: Natural History: A Selection*, trans. John H. Healy. New York: Penguin, 1991, p. 40.

21. Apollodorus, *Library*, excerpted in Rhoda A. Hendricks, ed. and trans., *Classical Gods and Heroes: Myths as Told by the Ancient Authors*. New York: Morrow Quill, 1974, p. 157.

22. Apollonius of Rhodes, *Argonautica*, trans. R.C. Seaton. Cambridge, MA: Harvard University Press, 1912, pp. 303, 305.

23. Pseudo-Hyginus, *Astronomica*, trans. Mary Grant, Theoi Greek Mythology. www.theoi.com.

24. Ovid, *Metamorphoses*, trans. A.D. Melville, excerpted in Theoi Greek Mythology, "Keto Aithiopios." www.theoi.com.

Chapter Four: Sinister Creatures with Women's Faces

25. Hesiod, *Theogony*, trans. H.G. Evelyn-White, p. 123.

26. Sabine McKellen, "Why Were Women a Necessary Evil in Greek Mythology?," Synonym. http://classroom.synonym.com.

27. Pseudo-Apollodorus, *Bibliotheca*.

28. Pseudo-Apollodorus, *Bibliotheca*.

29. Ovid, *Metamorphoses*, trans. Mary M. Innes. London: Penguin, 2006, p. 115.

30. Hesiod, *Theogony*, in Dorothea Wender, trans., *Hesiod and Theognis*. New York: Penguin, 1982, p. 32.

31. C.M. Bowra, *The Greek Experience*. New York: Barnes and Noble, 1996, p. 163.

32. Freeman, *The Greek Achievement*, p. 82.

33. Hesiod, *Theogony*, trans. Dorothea Wender, p. 239.

Chapter Five: Mythical Monsters in Modern Culture

34. Matt Kaplan, "The Science of Monsters," ABC Science, 2015. www.abc.net.au.

35. Jon Solomon, *The Ancient World in the Cinema*. New Haven, CT: Yale University Press, 2001, p. 115.

36. Solomon, *The Ancient World in the Cinema*, p. 102.

For Further Research

Books

Apollonius of Rhodes, *Argonautica*, trans. Aaron Poochigian. New York: Penguin, 2014.

Jason Colavito, *Jason and the Argonauts Through the Ages*. Jefferson, NC: McFarland, 2014.

Tony Dalton, *Ray Harryhausen: A Life in Pictures*. London: Ray and Diana Harryhausen Foundation, 2014.

Kathleen N. Daly, *Greek and Roman Mythology A to Z*. New York: Chelsea House, 2009.

Bernard Evslin, *Monsters of Greek Mythology*. New York: Open Road Media, 2014.

Michael Ford and Eoin Coveney, *Heroes, Gods, and Monsters of Ancient Greek Mythology*. St. Louis, MO: Book House, 2015.

Edith Hamilton, *Mythology*. New York: Grand Central, 2011.

Charles Kingsley, *The Heroes*. Santa Barbara, CA: Mission Audio, 2011.

Mark P.O. Morford and Robert J. Lenardon, *Classical Mythology*. New York: Oxford University Press, 2010.

Internet Sources

Classical Wisdom Weekly, "The Ten Most Terrifying Monsters of Greek Mythology," October 31, 2013. http://classicalwisdom.com/top-ten-terrifying-monsters-greek-mythology.

Hellenic Times, "Beasts of Greek Mythology," 2011. www.thehellenictimes.com/beasts.html.

Matt Kaplan, "The Science of Monsters," ABC Science, 2015. www
.abc.net.au/science/articles/2013/07/08/3795976.htm.

Paleothea, "Monstresses and Monstrosities." www.paleothea.com
/LadyMonsters.html.

Websites

Greek Mythology Link (www.maicar.com/GML/index.html). This
well-thought-out site has a biographical dictionary with more than
six thousand entries and some forty-five hundred photos, drawings,
and other images.

Medea's Lair: Tales of Greek Mythology (www.medeaslair.net
/myths.html). The authors of this site do a nice job of retelling the old
myths, which are grouped into categories that include "Men and Heroes," "Tales of Love and Loss," and "Giants and Beasts."

Mythweb Encyclopedia of Greek Mythology (www.mythweb.com
/encyc). This website provides a lot of useful information about both
major and minor Greek mythological characters.

Theoi Greek Mythology (www.theoi.com). This is the most compre-
hensive and reliable general website about Greek mythology on the
Internet. It features hundreds of separate pages filled with detailed,
accurate information, as well as numerous primary sources.

Index

Picture Credits

About the Author

Classical historian Don Nardo has written numerous acclaimed volumes about ancient civilizations and peoples. They include more than a dozen overviews of the mythologies of the Sumerians, Babylonians, Egyptians, Greeks, Romans, Persians, and others. Nardo also composes and arranges orchestral music. He lives with his wife, Christine, in Massachusetts.